BE A SCIENTIST

LET'S INVESTIGATE MAGNETS

JACQUI BAILEY

CRABTREE
PUBLISHING COMPANY
WWW.CRABTREEBOOKS.COM

CRABTREE
PUBLISHING COMPANY
WWW.CRABTREEBOOKS.COM

Author: Jacqui Bailey

Editorial director: Kathy Middleton

Series editor: Julia Bird

Editor: Ellen Rodger

Illustrator: Ed Myer

Packaged by: Collaborate

Proofreader: Petrice Custance

**Production coordinator
and Prepress technician:** Ken Wright

Print coordinator: Katherine Berti

Library and Achives Canada Cataloguing in Publication

Title: Let's investigate magnets / Jacqui Bailey.
Other titles: Investigating magnets
Names: Bailey, Jacqui, author.
Description: Series statement: Be a scientist |
  Previously published under title: Investigating magnets. |
  Includes index.
Identifiers: Canadiana (print) 20200354523 |
  Canadiana (ebook) 20200354531 |
  ISBN 9781427127747 (hardcover) |
  ISBN 9781427127808 (softcover) |
  ISBN 9781427127860 (HTML)
Subjects: LCSH: Magnets—Juvenile literature. |
  LCSH: Magnets—Experiments—Juvenile literature.
Classification: LCC QC757.5 .B35 2021 | DDC j538/.4   dc23

Library of Congress Cataloging-in-Publication Data

Names: Bailey, Jacqui, author.
Title: Let's investigate magnets / Jacqui Bailey.
Description: New York, NY : Crabtree Publishing Company, 2021. |
  Series: Be a scientist | Includes index.
Identifiers: LCCN 2020045093 (print) |
  LCCN 2020045094 (ebook) |
  ISBN 9781427127747 (hardcover) |
  ISBN 9781427127808 (paperback) |
  ISBN 9781427127860 (ebook)
Subjects: LCSH: Magnets--Juvenile literature.
Classification: LCC QC757.5 .B347 2021 (print) |
  LCC QC757.5 (ebook) | DDC 538/.4--dc23
LC record available at https://lccn.loc.gov/2020045093
LC ebook record available at https://lccn.loc.gov/2020045094

Crabtree Publishing Company

www.crabtreebooks.com   1–800–387–7650
Published in 2021 by Crabtree Publishing Company

First published in Great Britain in 2019 by Wayland
Copyright © Hodder & Stoughton, 2019

The text in this book was previously published
in the series 'Investigating Science'

Printed in the U.S.A./122020/CG20201014

Every attempt has been made to clear copyright.
Should there be any inadvertent omission please apply
to the publisher for rectification.

Published in Canada
Crabtree Publishing
616 Welland Ave.
St. Catharines, Ontario
L2M 5V6

Published in the United States
Crabtree Publishing
347 Fifth Avenue
Suite 1402–145
New York, NY 10016

BE A SCIENTIST

LET'S INVESTIGATE MAGNETS

CRABTREE
PUBLISHING COMPANY
WWW.CRABTREEBOOKS.COM

CONTENTS

WHAT ARE MAGNETS?

Magnets are pieces of metal or stone that can make things stick to them.

THINK about the kinds of magnets you may have seen.
- Magnets come in all shapes and sizes.
- Some toys have magnets in them.

YOU WILL NEED
Scissors
Some string
A long pencil
A donut magnet
Colored cardboard or construction paper
A permanent marker
Some metal paper clips

WHAT DO MAGNETS DO?

1 Cut a length of string longer than your pencil. Tie one end to the pencil and the other end to the magnet. This is your fishing rod.

2 Cut some fish shapes out of the cardboard or paper. Number each fish. Attach a paper clip to each fish.

3 Put the fish on the ground or in a large bowl.

4 Lower the magnet over the fish. Can you catch any fish? If you play with a friend you can take turns fishing. When all the fish have been caught, add up the numbers of your catch and see who has the highest score.

"

BECAUSE...

The paper clip on the fish sticks to the magnet, so the magnet is able to pull the fish off the ground. This is because the magnet is pulling the metal paper clip toward it. Most magnets are made of the metals iron or **steel**. There is also a magnetic rock called **lodestone** (left) or magnetite.

"

MAGNETIC MATERIALS

Some objects stick to magnets and others do not.

THINK about where you would find magnets in your home.
• Fridge doors have small magnets in them to hold the door shut
• Fridge magnets can decorate the fridge door.

What sort of objects stick to magnets?

OBJECT	GUESS	RESULT
coin		
eraser		
key		

WHICH MATERIALS ARE MAGNETIC?

1 Use the pencil and ruler to divide your paper into three columns. Label each column as shown above.

2 Write a list of your test objects in the first column.

3 In the second column, checkmark the objects you think will stick to the magnet. Put a cross next to those you think will not.

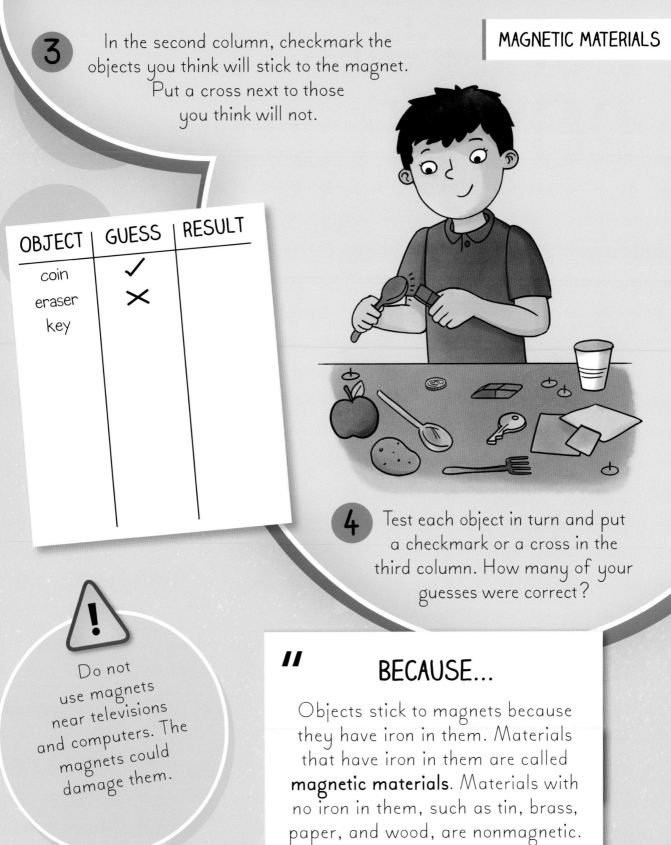

OBJECT	GUESS	RESULT
coin	✓	
eraser	✗	
key		

4 Test each object in turn and put a checkmark or a cross in the third column. How many of your guesses were correct?

⚠ Do not use magnets near televisions and computers. The magnets could damage them.

" BECAUSE...

Objects stick to magnets because they have iron in them. Materials that have iron in them are called **magnetic materials**. Materials with no iron in them, such as tin, brass, paper, and wood, are nonmagnetic. They do not stick to magnets. **"**

9

PULLING POWER

A **force** is a pull or push. The pulling power of magnets is a force called **magnetism.**

THINK about different kinds of force.
• You lift a glass using the force of your muscles.
• A magnet pulls on a paper clip using magnetism.

Can you see magnetism work?

YOU WILL NEED
A pen and a ruler
A piece of paper
A strong bar magnet
Some paper clips
A horseshoe magnet

HOW DOES MAGNETISM WORK?

1 Use the ruler to draw a straight line along the long edge of the paper. Draw a line at each 0.5-inch (1.27 cm) mark until you reach 5 inches (12.7 cm), as shown at left.

2 Draw a line across the page at the 5-inch (12.7 cm) and 0.5-inch (1.27 cm) marks, as shown at right. These are the start and finish lines.

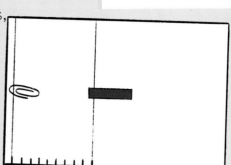

3 Place the bar magnet on the start line and the paper clip on the finish line.

4 Slowly slide the bar magnet along the paper toward the paper clip. How far away is the magnet from the paper clip before anything happens?

5 Try the test again, using the horseshoe magnet instead of the bar magnet. What happens?

" BECAUSE...

The paper clip moves toward the magnet because it is **attracted**, or pulled, to the magnet by the force of magnetism. Magnets have different strengths. How far away the magnet is before it attracts the paper clip depends on the strength of your magnet. "

POLES APART

Magnetism is stronger at the ends of a magnet than in the middle.

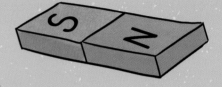

THINK about a bar magnet.
- The ends of a magnet are known as its **poles**.
- Sometimes the poles are different colors. They may also be marked with the letters "N" and "S" for north and south pole.

How are the poles of a magnet different?

YOU WILL NEED
Some tape
2 toy cars
2 bar magnets
(at least as long as the cars)

WHAT HAPPENS WHEN DIFFERENT POLES TOUCH?

1 Tape the middle of each magnet to the roof of a toy car. Make sure both magnets have the same pole pointing to the front of the car.

2 What happens when you push the front of one car towards the back of the other?

3 What happens when you push both cars face-to-face?

4 What happens if you put the cars back-to-back?

BECAUSE...

When one car is behind the other, the magnets pull the cars together. This is because the opposite poles are facing each other (north to south, or south to north). Opposite magnetic poles attract each other. When the two cars are facing each other or when they are back-to-back, the magnets push the cars apart. This is because the same poles are facing each other (north to north or south to south). The same magnetic poles **repel**, or push away from, each other.

AN INVISIBLE FORCE

Magnetism is an invisible force – you cannot see it. It can pull on things without touching them.

THINK about how magnetism works.
- The paper clip on pages 10–11 jumped toward the magnet before the magnet touched it.
- Magnetism can reach through the air to pull on something.

How far does magnetism reach?

YOU WILL NEED
Plastic wrap
A bar magnet
A disc magnet
A jar of iron filings (or steel wool chopped into small pieces)
A piece of paper

HOW DOES MAGNETISM SURROUND A MAGNET?

1 Wrap both magnets in plastic wrap. Place the paper on top of the bar magnet, so that the magnet is in the middle.

2 Sprinkle the iron filings (or steel wool) onto the paper, around the spot where the magnet is. What happens?

3 Lift the paper up and carefully pour your filings back into the jar.

4 Replace the bar magnet with the disc magnet. Shake the filings onto the paper again. What happens this time?

BECAUSE...

" The iron filings form lines on the paper showing how the magnetic force, or magnetism, pulls the iron filings toward the magnet. Different-shaped magnets make different patterns. The filings are usually thickest at the poles, but other lines spread out from the magnet, or curve from pole to pole. These lines show how far from the magnet its magnetic force reaches. This area is called its **magnetic field.** "

STRENGTH OF FORCE

A magnetic field can reach through nonmagnetic materials.

THINK about what fridge magnets do.

- A fridge magnet will hold a piece of paper on to a magnetic surface, such as a metal door.
- But paper is nonmagnetic and will not stick to the magnet on its own.

How strong is a magnetic field?

YOU WILL NEED
Scissors
Paper
A bar magnet
Tape
A paper clip

HOW STRONG IS A MAGNETIC FIELD?

1 Cut the paper into several squares. Make the squares large enough to wrap around the magnet.

2 Check that the magnet is strong enough to pick up the paper clip.

3 Wrap the magnet in one layer of paper and pick up the paper clip.

4 Repeat step 3 a number of times, adding an extra layer of paper each time.

5 How do the different layers of paper affect the magnet?

"
BECAUSE...
The magnet should pick up the paper clip through at least one layer. This is because its magnetic force spreads outwards, as we saw on pages 14-15. If the magnet is wrapped in several layers of paper, the layers will gradually block the magnetic force and the magnet will no longer work.
"

17

MAGNETIC MAGIC

Magnetism can work through most materials, including water.

THINK about what water is.
- Everything in the world is made of some kind of material.
- Water is a liquid material. It flows in streams, rivers, lakes, and oceans.

Can you use a magnet to pull something out of water?

YOU WILL NEED

A glass jar
Water
A paper clip
A magnet
Some string

DO MAGNETS WORK THROUGH WATER?

1 Almost fill the glass jar with water.

2 Drop the paper clip in and let it sink to the bottom of the jar.

" BECAUSE...

You can use the magnet to slide the paper clip up the side of the glass jar because its magnetic field passes through the glass and the water to pull on the paper clip. If you put the magnet into the water it will still work on the paper clip because water is nonmagnetic and does not block the magnetic field. "

4 Repeat step 2, but this time tie a length of string around the magnet and lower it into the water. Will it pick up the paper clip?

3 What happens if you hold the magnet to the outside of the jar near the paper clip? Can you make the paper clip move? Can you lift it to the top of the jar?

MOVING WITH MAGNETS

The pulling power of magnets can be used in different ways.

THINK about how magnets are used to move things.

• A crane with a large magnet hanging from it is used to lift and move heavy blocks of metal in a scrap yard.

How can you use magnets?

YOU WILL NEED

A permanent marker

A large piece of stiff cardboard

2 square pieces of thin cardstock paper

4 food cans

2 paper clips

2 disc magnets

2 rulers

Tape

Scissors

A watch

CAN YOU MAKE A MAGNETIC GAME?

1   Use the permanent marker to draw a wiggly road on the large piece of cardboard.

2 Make a fold across the middle of each thin piece of cardstock. Draw and cut out the shape of a car on the paper above the fold. Cut the fold into two flaps and fold them in opposite directions so that the car stands upright. Repeat these steps to make a second car.

3 Prop up the large piece of cardboard with a can at each corner so there is a clear gap beneath it. Slide a paper clip onto the front flap of each car and place the cars at the start of the road.

4 Tape a magnet to the end of each ruler and slide the magnets underneath the cardboard road to move the cars. How long does it take each player to move their car to the end of the road?

BECAUSE...

The magnets are able to move the cars around the road because their magnetic force passes through the cardboard and attracts the metal paper clips attached to the cars.

21

SORTING WITH MAGNETS

Magnets can be used to separate some materials from others.

THINK about how magnets are used to separate things.

• Magnets separate iron and steel from other materials in a scrapyard.

• Iron and steel are often recycled, or reused. Magnets separate steel cans from aluminum cans so they can be recycled.

Why not make your own can sorter?

YOU WILL NEED

Some string

A strong magnet

Some clean, empty food and soda cans

WHAT KIND OF METAL IS IT?

1 Tie a length of string as long as your leg to the magnet.

2 Stand the cans in a line on the floor.

3 Hold the string in your hand and let the magnet dangle over the cans. Slowly move it along the line of cans. What happens? Which cans are attracted to the magnet, and which ones are not?

" BECAUSE...

Some of the cans will be attracted to the magnet, but others will not. This is because some cans are made of steel, which is a magnetic material, and some are made of aluminum, which is a nonmagnetic material. Which types of food and drink are stored in steel cans and which types are stored in aluminum cans? "

FLOATING WITH MAGNETS

The pushing force of magnets is also useful.

THINK about how magnets repel each other.

• The cars on pages 12-13 repelled each other when they were facing back-to-back.

Can you use this pushing force to make a magnet float?

YOU WILL NEED
3 donut magnets
Colored paper
Scissors
A glue stick
or tape
A small wooden dowel almost as thick as the hole in the magnets
Modeling clay

HOW CAN YOU MAKE MAGNETS FLOAT?

1 Find out which side of your magnets stick together. As opposite poles attract, one side will be a north pole, the other a south pole.

2 Cut out and glue or tape a small square of colored paper onto the north side of each magnet.

BECACAUSE...

"

The magnets float apart because they all have the same poles facing each other. North-to-north or south-to-south poles repel each other. Without the dowel, the magnets would slip sideways and drop to the table. The rod holds them in place, keeping the poles facing each other.

"

Push the dowel into a lump of modeling clay so that it stands upright.

4 Slide magnet 1 onto the dowel north-side up. Slide magnet 2 north-side down, and magnet 3 north-side up. What happens to the magnets?

POINTING THE WAY

A **compass** helps people to find their way from place to place. Magnets have been used in compasses for hundreds of years.

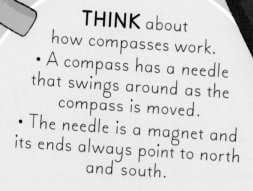

THINK about how compasses work.
- A compass has a needle that swings around as the compass is moved.
- The needle is a magnet and its ends always point to north and south.

How can you make a magnet work like a compass?

HOW DOES A COMPASS WORK?

1 Tape the sheet of paper onto a tabletop or the floor.

2 Tie one end of the string around the middle of the bar magnet so that it balances when you hold it out.

YOU WILL NEED
A piece of paper
Tape
A length of string
A bar magnet
A pen and a ruler
A pocket compass
(keep this well away from the bar magnet)

3 Dangle the magnet just above the paper and keep your hand still. When the magnet stops moving it will point in a particular direction.

4 Carefully lower the magnet onto the paper. Without moving the magnet, mark where the two poles of the magnet lie on the paper.

5 Remove the magnet and use a ruler to draw a line through the middle of the two marks. Place your compass on top of the line. How does your line compare with the compass needle?

" BECAUSE...

The magnet line and the compass needle point in the same direction. This is because the bar magnet and the compass needle are lining up with Earth's magnetic poles. Earth itself is a giant magnet. Its magnetic poles are near to Earth's North Pole and South Pole. "

GLOSSARY

Attract
is what a magnet does when it pulls something toward it. Attract is the opposite of repel.

Compass
is an instrument that tells you in which direction north and south are, no matter where you are on Earth's surface. Some compasses work only in the northern hemisphere. This is the part of Earth north of the equator. Others work only in the southern hemisphere, or south of the equator..

Force
is a scientific word for a push or pull. A force makes an object move in a particular direction. It can also change a moving object's direction, slow it down, or speed it up. Magnetism is a force.

Lodestone
is a type of rock that is naturally magnetic. More than 1,000 years ago, people in ancient China used lodestones as compasses. A lodestone is also called magnetite.

Magnetic field
is the area surrounding a magnet within which its magnetic force will work. When a magnetic material comes within reach of a magnetic field, it is pulled toward the magnet inside that field.

Earth is surrounded by its own magnetic field. This is because the center of Earth is made of iron and it acts like a giant magnet.

Magnetic materials

are those materials that are attracted to magnets. Any material that has iron in it is a magnetic material.

Magnetism

is the pulling or pushing force that a magnet has.

Poles

are the two ends of a magnet. Magnetism is strongest at the poles. On a disc magnet the poles are its two flat faces.

Repel

is what a magnet does when it pushes another magnet away from it.

Steel

is a metal made from iron. Iron is found in the ground, in rocks called ore.

A piece of metal can be made to work like a magnet by sending electricity through it. This type of magnet is called an electromagnet. Electromagnets work only while electricity is flowing through them. When the electricity is switched off, the magnet stops working.

A special type of train, called a Maglev train, speeds along on a cushion of air instead of wheels. Strong magnets laid on the track repel other magnets under the train and lift the carriages into the air.

LEARNING MORE

BOOKS

Arnold, Nick. *Forces of Nature: Experiments with Forces and Magnetism.* Quarto Publishing Group, 2019.

Claybourne, Anna. *Recreate Discoveries About Forces.* Crabtree Publishing, 2019.

Spilsbury, Richard. *Investigating Magnetism.* Crabtree Publishing, 2018.

WEBSITES

Visit this site for some cool magnet facts:
www.coolkidfacts.com/magnetism-facts-for-kids/

www.dkfindout.com/uk/science/magnets/ has lots of helpful information on magnetic objects. It also includes a quiz.

PLACES TO VISIT

The Exploratorium in San Francisco, California, is a public learning laboratory that people can visit. It also has online exhibits on magnetism you can access at: www.exploratorium.edu/exhibits/subject/electricity-and-magnetism.

NOTE TO PARENTS AND TEACHERS:

Every effort has been made by the publisher to ensure that these websites contain no inappropriate or offensive material. However, because of the nature of the Internet, it is impossible to guarantee that the content of these sites will not be altered. We strongly advise that Internet access is supervised by a responsible adult.

INDEX

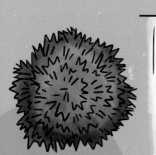